I Am A Writer An. Say Or Do May Be Used In A Story

CREATIVE'S COMPOSITION NOTEBOOK FOR JOURNALING AND DAILY WRITING

STUART CLARKE

GINZBURG PRESS

Copyright © 2018 by Ginzburg Press

All rights reserved. No part of this publication may be reproduced, distributed or transmitted in any form or by any means, including photocopying, recording, or other electronic or mechanical methods, without the prior written permission of the publisher, except in the case of brief quotations embodied in critical reviews and certain other noncommercial uses permitted by copyright law.

www.ginzburgpress.com

Made in United States
North Haven, CT
12 October 2023

42664270R00083